PAIN IS NOT OUR ONLY PAINTBRUSH

TERRANCE P. **ELMORE**

Copyright © 2023 Terrance P. Elmore

All rights reserved. This book or any portion thereof may not be reproduced or used in any manner whatsoever without the express written permission of the publisher except for the use of brief quotations in a book review.

Printed in the United States of America

First Printing 2023

ISBN: 978-0-9897328-6-4

Library of Congress Control Number: 2023915880

Back and interior photos by Your World On Film

Published by

Truly In His Hands
Goose Creek, SC

For Nicole

Dedicated to everyone on a journey to spread love in
a world that seems to be full of hate.

Contents

Introduction 7

Familiar Fruit 11
History in the Making 12
Manhood 14
House of Cards 16
Masculinity 17
Brothers 18
Slow Burn 20
Man Enough 22
Windows 24
Happiness 26
Uncaged and Unclipped 28
We Rise 29
Thoughts 30
Weighted Words 32
If Not Us, Then Who? 34
Walk it Off 36
Skin 37
Abundance 39
Chapters of Joy 41
Our Spirit 42
Bootstraps 43
Wildflowers 45
Summertime 46
Dandelion 48
Weeds 49
Tragedy 50
Reflections 52
Potential 54

Struggle	56
Unpolished	58
Flaws	60
Abundantly	62
The Past	64
Unbeatable	66
Beautiful	68
Chapters	70
Mahogany Smile	72
Herbal Tea	73
Juneteenth	74
Black Sheep	76
How to Start Healing	79
What If?	82
Emancipation	85
Possible Thoughts	86
I Wonder	88
A Poem for Tomorrow, Today	90
Black Love	93
Resilient	96
Our Excellence Is Everywhere	97
Touch the Stars	98
Discovery	99
Echoes of the Past	100
Walk it Off (Keep Going)	102
Black Owned	104
Plentiful Fruit	107
About the Author	108

Introduction

When I began writing this book, I was inspired to write something with a different tone but the same message as my first two books. At the time when I decided to write my first two books, I grew tired of seeing negative depictions of love and being in love. The idea that love is pain was echoing aimlessly throughout timelines without any accountability to the real problem, people who mishandle and misrepresent love. I was tired of seeing painful and traumatic stories being highlighted as Black stories when I decided to write this book. Yes, those stories are important and necessary to share, but what about the rest of our stories?

I've been all too familiar with police brutality and fatalities. Growing up I was taught that a routine police stop is ten times out of ten less likely to be in my favor. Reaching for my proof of insurance and registration could be my death warrant or close enough to it. The first time I learned this was in 1991 when video surfaced of four police officers beating an unarmed Rodney King almost to death. The following year these officers were acquitted, and my young mind caught a glimpse into the depths of hatred and the layers of racism. And along with the rest of the world I witnessed the aftermath of injustice as people took to the streets of Los Angeles and began to riot. Why were the people so angry that they would destroy their own neighborhoods? A question I asked myself but wouldn't get the answer to until I became an adult.

Since the Rodney King video I've seen countless more that affected me in their own way, but none affected me the way George Floyd's video did. I still haven't brought myself to watch the entire eight minutes and 46 seconds, and probably never will, but the minutes I did watch were enough for me feel a new level of sadness, grief, and anger. The cry for Black Lives to matter started growing louder and my book began to take on a new direction. The song "Strange Fruit" played on repeat in my mind and writing became my best option for a healthy outlet. So, I began writing my version and called it "Familiar Fruit". In fact, I wrote several poems to express my feelings towards the injustices I've witnessed and experienced.

The more I wrote the more I realized what was intended to be an inspiring book was turning into a book filled with stories of pain and trauma. The type of stories that get the most attention and mentions.

With this, the direction of my book changed again. This time for good. I decided this book would be filled with positive Black stories that will inspire anyone who reads it. I no longer wanted to share "Familiar Fruit" but a conversation with my wife and mother changed my mind. They both agreed that I should include the poem since the rest of the book is filled with poems that go in such a better direction. I'm on a journey to spread love in a world that seems to be filled with hate and this book is another contribution to this journey.

Terrance P. Elmore

Familiar Fruit

Strange fruits no longer hang in the poplar trees,
they've become familiar fruits
—harvested on the ground.

The streets bare a familiar fruit
Blood on the concrete and blood shed with ill repute
Black bodies cut down like annual weeds
This familiar fruit streaming on the popular feeds

Liberty and justice for all
"Accidentally" shot even when you made the call
Facades of equality sweet and fresh
Then the sudden stench of another unarmed Black death

Here's another fruit plucked too soon
Another peeled rind for the compost
Another fruit-bearing tree that won't reach its bloom
Leaves withered and branches lopped
Here is a familiar and spoiled crop

History in the Making

Black history is American history
in the making every day.

Painted on the canvas
of a land where we
touched the soil
and made it rich.

Continuously cultivating
and always thriving.

A culture making influences
that reach places where
the hues aren't welcomed.

Pain is not our only paintbrush.
Our canvases aren't always
woven in

**trauma,
suffering,
and
violence.**

Our true Canvases are worthy
to don gallery walls.

As permanent exhibitions where
hope,
happiness,
and, *compassion*

are always on full display.

Drawn in a sea of endless sketch books
are portraits of fathers teaching their sons
how to set sails into the voyages of manhood.

Created from pencils with
different grades of toughness.
Each one with its individual purpose.
Each one as important as the next.

Every opportunity taken to
sharpen our dullness reveals
a fresh and vibrant core.

We use multiple mediums
to share stories of
all things beautiful.

Priceless masterpieces
displayed for the world to see.
We're history in the making every day.

Manhood

Every day we
navigate through the
labyrinth of manhood.

Unable to locate a map
or borrow one from
the fathers who are still
piecing together their own.

We stumble through
the same way they
stumbled before us.

Sometimes walking into walls
mistaking them for pathways.

Sometimes walking down dead-end
pathways mistaking them for a way out.

Through the frustration and confusion,
we learn which turns we must make
and which ones we must avoid.

With every misstep and setback,
we understand more that manhood
is learning from the mistakes of the past
in order to move into the future.

Without fully understanding the assignment,
we learned how to become men by instructing
ourselves.

> We learned from our individual mistakes
> and took notes from each other's.

Unqualified and underexperienced
we put together faulty lesson plans
and fumbled through flawed curriculums.

Thinking that when we became adults,
we would have it all figured out.
> As if getting older is an automatic rite of passage.
> A certification signifying achievement
> and a successful completion of boyhood.

> We learned how to become men

through the guidance of each other.
Observing all of the wrong ways,
we eventually came up with
a plan

to get it right.

House of Cards

Empathetic to the hands
we were dealt because
we've seen the deck
from which they came.

Promising ourselves we
won't deal
the same hands.

Worn and faded decks
with folded corners.

A few unidentified stains
with stories to tell.

Through it all,
these less than perfect
cards still hold winning hands.

Masculinity

True masculinity doesn't thrive
with the absence of femininity.

Toxicity is the absence of unity.
Toxicity is the absence of balance.
Toxicity is the absence of love.

True masculinity is the presence of *femininity*.

Brothers

Brothers aren't always
forged through blood.

Sometimes the connection
of **brotherhood** is
what forms bonds.

A **brother** is someone who
knows you better than
you know yourself.

A **brother** is someone who
keeps you accountable.

A **brother** doesn't let you fall.

Even though we may stumble
and sometimes fall...
A **brother** is there without judgement
to pick you up.

A **brother** is someone who
rides with you when necessary, but
stops you from taking the wrong path.

A **brother** is someone who
will always be there,
no matter what.

Even if being there
means showing up

      f r o m   a   d i s t a n c e .

No matter how much time passes,

                         brothers will always pick up
                         right where we left off.

Slow Burn

With our burdens on one shoulder
and the world on the other,
we carry our families on our backs.

Without pausing to process
our thoughts
to evaluate our emotions,
we cover our families with everything
we have.

Focused on putting out fires-
it's easy to ignore the ambers
that have attached themselves.

A slow burn of life's harshness and cruelty.

Unknowingly awaiting
an accelerant to
ignite the flames.

Lessons learned from mistakes made.

Terrance P. Elmore

A tower of building blocks
stacked to near perfection.

Many failed attempts
taught the importance of
a solid foundation.

Strides made from the rear.

Fighting every step
along the way to make every
disadvantage an advantage.

Man Enough

Man enough to know that
it's okay to not always be okay.

Strength is acknowledging
where I am at that moment.

Acknowledging and embracing
all of my emotions.

Man enough to know that
she doesn't always need
me to be her hero.

Sometimes she just needs
me to
listen as a friend.

Man enough to know that
it's okay to admit
when I make mistakes.

Perfection is unrealistic pressure
with real burdens and stress.

Man enough to know that
I won't win every fight,
but the courage to know
which things are worth fighting for.

Man enough to know that
I can pause, when necessary,
but I have to keep going.

Man enough to know that
being a man is more about
what I do with gentleness
than with strength.

Man enough to know that
vulnerability is a part of growth
and a real sign of strength.

Man enough to know that
just being a man **isn't enough.**

Windows

If it's true that our eyes are
the windows to our souls,
then our smiles must be
the windows to our hearts.

> What do we see when
> we look in the mirror?
> What do we see when
> we look in the mirror?

What makes us smile
back at ourselves with
so much freedom and
joy?

We can only imagine
what people see when
we draw back the curtains
and allow them a peek inside.

We hope and pray that they
see the nature of our hearts.

Filled with love for
ourselves,
family,
and
communities.

Empathetic to challenges that
may not match our own.

Not because life is easy,
but because we realize
how precious life truly is.

Happiness

Happiness comes from

    a place where the sun

        shines on a cloudy day

and the rain is a mist

    that replenishes

        our spirit.

It comes from a place where

springtime lasts forever and

grace blooms in self-love.   Happiness comes from

a place where affirmations

whisper to our hearts like

a gentle breeze and life is

the berry patch of choices

—with no regrets

Uncaged and Unclipped

Believing that we can fly isn't limited to
whether or not we were born with wings.

It's our unlimited belief that makes it possible.

Whether are not we are born with wings,
we willingly clip them with disbelief.

The flight pattern of believing in
ourselves being the most difficult.

Elevated beyond the sky.

We were born to fly.

Uncaged
and
unclipped.

We Rise

It's funny how we'd rather
believe the lies we can't see
than believe the evidence that's
gotten us from point A to B.

Working overtime to discredit
the progress we've made.

One mistake.
That's all it takes for us to
turn thousands of steps of progress
into a deepfake memory.

Diminishing the triumphs of our past
we remove ourselves from first place to last.

Still, we rise as champions,
moving forward in victory.

Facing every challenge,
making our mark

in history.

Thoughts

> Sometimes the sharpest minds
> can become prisoners
> to their thoughts.

>> Becoming empty hallways
>> filled with the hollow echoes
>> of doubt and regret.

> A lonely place with
> unmarked doors that
> make it seem inescapable.

>> It isn't until we realize that
>> we've created this space so
>> we know how to exit back
>> into a place of peace.

The doors are unmarked
because we already have
the key to unlock each one.

                    It feels lonely because
                    we haven't let anyone in.

Our thoughts were never
intended to hold us captive.

                    Our thoughts should be
                    the balance that allows
                    our minds to be

free.

Weighted Words

Gardens filled with whatever our hearts desire.
Everything is up for the taking,
but yet we leave with empty terracotta pots.
One stacked on top of the other.
What 'could be' fitting into who we're afraid to be.

We were made for much more than
just getting by on the minimum.
Sometimes comfort makes us blind to the fact that
we are tethered to the essence of God.
Beautiful in His eyes we are destined for greatness,
poised for purpose, and equipped for the inevitable.

Even if we spent an eternity on this earth,
we would never reach the apex of our full potential.
In days past we've carried the heavy load of empty promises,
but on this day, we stack plans on top of actions.

Weighted words of life carry no burdens.
Complacency becomes an antiquity as we open our eyes and
see that everything we wanted and need was always
in proximity waiting for us to discover our worth.

If Not Us, Then Who?

If we allow fears to dictate our lives,
we will allow mediocrity to
become our level of expectation.

If we continue to second guess our ideas,
we will live as second best to only ourselves.

If we dream without action,
we will never reach any goals.

If we become discouraged because of a loss or two,
we will become complacent at living defeated.

If we stop reaching up for more,
our hands will remain empty and bounded by our sides.

If we are ok with just enough,
we will miss out on an exceeding abundance
in every area of our life.

If we don't fix or change what hasn't been working,
we will always be broken.

If we don't speak out and use our voice for change,
we will always live in the silence of 'what if'.

If we don't start now,
every day we'll be waiting for tomorrow.

If we don't believe in ourselves,
then who else will?

If Not Us, Then Who?

Walk it Off

Emotionally we walk with a limp because
we were told enough times when we fell to
get up and walk it off.

Ignoring the scratches and wounds.

Never examining the pain,
just walking through it and with it.

Limping unnoticed we
believe that everything is okay.

Until one day the limp becomes
a burdenous stagger throughout life.

Then help comes along
before the damage really sets in.

Therapeutic healing begins.
We learn how to walk it through.
We learn to talk it through.

Skin

Why am I
comfortable in my skin?
Because I know who I am
regardless of stereotypes
I didn't create.

Unafraid
to be
unapologetically
me.

Never leaving my confidence
in the opinion of those
too privileged to relate.

I love what I see when
I look in the mirror.
God's given purpose

For me to believe anything else
would be inferior.

A mantel of pride
built on the influence of
our grandparent's voices.

The reverb of excellence
and the echoes of forever
keep me comfortable
in my skin.

*My heart rejoices
every time I think about
the skin
that I'm in.*

Abundance

There's an abundance of joy.
I'm reminded of that
every day that I wake up.
Thankful to see another day
and thankful for new mercies.
Whether it's Monday or Saturday,
I'm grateful for this privilege of life.

There's an abundance of grace.
Not just for others
but for ourselves too.
Sometimes we make mistakes
and lose our way,
but we find our way back.
Sometimes we stumble,
but we get up
and we try again.

There's an abundance of love.
As harsh as the world seems,
there's a lot of love to give,
there's a lot of love to receive,
and there's a whole lot of love to go around.
But We must be willing to give it
so we may receive it.

There's an abundance of everything—we need.
Sometimes we're moving too fast to notice.
Sometimes we just need to pause
and appreciate what's all around us.
Sometimes all we have to do is be still
and be in the moment.

Chapters of Joy

It's easy to get caught up in
what we see until it becomes
the only version of the truth.

Seeing is believing, but
the layers aren't always
easy to peel back.

At least not all of
the important ones.

The truth is,
in our lifetime we may never
see the end of hashtags
trending in remembrance of...

But even though
these tragedies happen,
they aren't the final
or finishing stories.

**They're a few sentences
in a much larger book,
filled with chapters** of joy
and hope filled stories.

Our Spirit

I love the sound of laughter
in the midst of sorrow.

it is a reminder of the thing
that makes us who we are

-our spirit.

No matter how many times
it's battered and bruised,
our spirit can't be broken.

Our spirit cannot be destroyed.

Whenever we laugh,
we heal the bruises
and close the wounds.

The more we laugh
the more scars
began to fade.

Bootstraps

It's easy to look at everything
we've accomplished,
the odds we've beaten
and wonder if it's really difficult for
everyone else to do the same.

        Pulling yourself up by
        the bootstraps wasn't easy,
        but you did it.

So why can't they?

Imagine wishing you
could do the same except
you don't have any boots
        to pull up.

        Wishing there was some way to
        ease the discomfort beneath your feet
        every time you take a step.

Imagine not being able to
achieve more for yourself
and the ones you love.

> Not because you couldn't,
> but because no one ever
> showed you that you could.

Wildflowers

Some seeds can be planted anywhere, and they will thrive. Growing wild in the sun and free in the harshest of climates. Against all odds becoming who they are destined to be.

Summertime

While growing up, summertime meant
no more school or getting up early to catch the bus.
Excited about friends we only get to see in classes.
Looking back, I honestly don't know which was more exciting,
the first day of school or the last.

Summertime meant endless days of
visiting and spending more time with family.
Memories of great times we will never forget.
Whether your father's mother or your mother's mother,
grandma's house is where everybody met.
Where granddaddy told us stories that always
reminded us just how much we really haven't lived yet.

Summertime meant playing basketball
in the neighborhood or pick-up games in the park.
Playing when the sun was at its highest point to
playing in the rain if it was light enough.
Anything to ignite that spark.

Cookouts every other day.
Hamburgers, hotdogs, ribs,
and leg quarters on the grill.
Red rice, macaroni, baked beans,
and potato salad on chill.

The days were longer but somehow
the nights felt longer too.
As long as you could stay awake,
when it was summertime,
you did not have a bedtime and
gained some extra hours on your curfew.

Summertime represented a freedom
we sometimes don't allow ourselves as adults.
So, let's start enjoying life more.
Taking time to do what we love
and enjoying the results.

Dandelion

It's the untainted innocence of a child
that stumbles across dandelions
and collects a beautiful bouquet.

It's the taught influence of hate
that mows them down
into withered weeds.

Weeds

It's untainted innocence that stumbles across dandelions and collects beautiful bouquets.

It's taught ignorance and hate that cuts them down into withered weeds.

It's the unbroken spirit that sees sunshine beyond the clouds, even when the skies are gray.

It's untainted innocence that stumbles across dandelions and collects beautiful bouquets.

It's underestimated confidence that holds this collection high to put love on display.

It's uncensored freedom that crowns kings with influence and adorns queens with dignity.

It's untainted innocence that stumbles across dandelions and collects beautiful bouquets.

It's taught ignorance and hate that cuts them down into withered weeds.

Pain Is Not Our Only Paintbrush

Tragedy

Terrance P. Elmore

I don't know which is more tragic

Them not seeing our beauty
or us not seeing it

ourselves.

Reflections

What they see as threats
Of violence and confusion
Are self-reflections

Pain Is Not Our Only Paintbrush

Potential

imagine walking
through hallways filled with unlocked
doors of potential

but you never turn any
knobs or walk into any rooms

Struggle

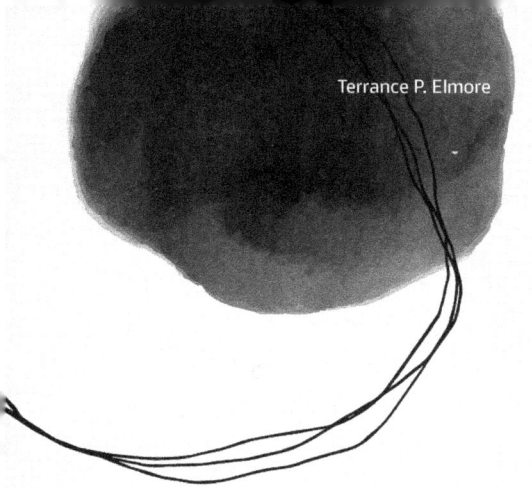

everyone's struggle
is different, but we all
must face at least one

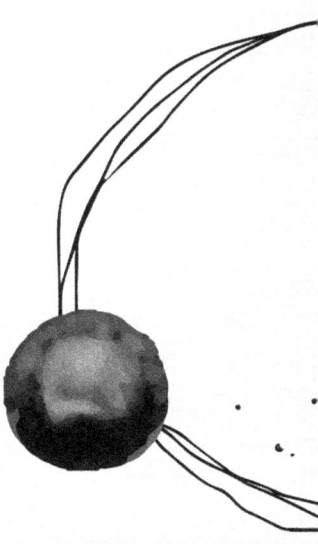

Pain Is Not Our Only Paintbrush

Unpolished

Terrance P. Elmore

beneath polished and almost perfected images are essential rough drafts

Pain Is Not Our Only Paintbrush

Flaws

Flaws
are beautiful
reminders of how

being unique is
perfect
imperfection.

Pain Is Not Our Only Paintbrush

Abund

*purpose
becomes abundantly
clear while trusting
God without limiting our*

f a i t h

Pain Is Not Our Only Paintbrush

The Past

embrace
the past
but only to
make room for the
future

Pain Is Not Our Only Paintbrush

Unbeatable

wake up with purpose
and go throughout your day
with unbeatable joy

Pain Is Not Our Only Paintbrush

Beautiful

Even
with all
of its scars
and bruises, life is
beautiful.

Chapters

Terrance P. Elmore

last
chapters aren't
final chapters if
you read between the

LIES

Mahogany Smile

Instead of turning our smiles
upside down,
we took the barrel,
stood on it,
and made it our podium.

On it we stand **tall**.

Smiles,

grins,

laughs

and all.

Herbal Tea

The temperature of our voices
are reaching a **boiling** point
as we prepare our empty cups.

Life's kettle screeches with
an undying call of readiness.

Loose leaves awaiting
the infusion of our
plans with action.

A Robust representation of
excellence is poured.

Juneteenth

It's heavy to be a father tasked with
the extra responsibility of making sure
our sons understand that:
freedom isn't the same for everyone.

But years of training have prepared us to
lift and effortlessly carry the weight.
While acknowledging that no matter how much
we prepare them it may not be enough.

Be proud anyway because the color of your skin isn't a determination of guilt.

Be who you were born
to be anyway because
you're not responsible for
prejudged [prejudiced] pictures of
who they want you to be.

It gets tiresome and frustrating
but don't let anger harden your heart.
Let it be the fuel that ignites you to
educate the ignorant,
baffle the bigots, and
debunk the demented.

Freedom may be different
on the soil but understand
there's a renaissance in our thoughts,
unwavering resilience in our hearts,
and revolution in the freedom of our voice.

**The only difference that matters
is who we honor with purpose
and represent with excellence.**

Black Sheep

Wondering what the path looks like
in this direction or that direction.
Curiosity set you on a path of your own.

Seen to the rest of the flock
as wandering
away.

But that would imply
aimlessness or carelessness
in the chosen path.

Your path was guided by
the journey of self-discovery.

Curiosity became the compass
that helped you find your way.

Always different,
but never inferior.

Always a loner,
but never alone.

Often indifferent,
but never insignificant.

Often misunderstood,
but never misleading.

A rouge willing to
rethink the rules.

A hero hell-bent on
learning their own way
—even if it's the hard way.

A trailblazer that's passed
every trial by fire.

Thought to be invaluable
because your complexion
wasn't the preferred hue.

Considered an anomaly
because of the complexity
in your nonconformity.

An unaltered original that's
always been recognized commercially
for your beauty.

Unreached and unrecognized levels
of power because being different
was considered
deficient.

A minority holding the majority of influence.

The most desired and sought after.

A leader in a crowd of followers.

A standout in a crowd of standstills.

Seen as an underdog but always recognized as champion.

How to Start Healing

Carrying around the weight
of all your burdens begins
to feel like dragging an
overstuffed backpack
through desert sand.

Sinking slowly, you only

notice when it's almost

sunken beneath the surface.

Pain Is Not Our Only Paintbrush

Unable to continue pulling the load, you look around and see that you are

knee-deep in sinking sand.

That's when you find a pen and it becomes your shovel. That's when you begin writing.

Terrance P. Elmore

Each word digs you more
and more out of the hole.
With each sentence, you wiggle
your way closer to freedom.
As you dig the backpack
begins unpacking. The load
gets lighter and it becomes
easier and easier to **write**.

Recused from the weight of your
burdens and sinking sand,
you start a new journey.
Solid ground under your feet
and an empty backpack
on your shoulders.

What If?

The cold and empty place
where you found solace
would no longer exist.
The complexity of communicating
in relationships would become
a seamless as saying hello.
Still unperfected but equipped.

What if you were allowed to
become a man instead of
being forced to be one?
Growing up before you've
outgrown your shoes.
Replacing them for
ones a few sizes too big.
—making it difficult to walk.

A hero would emerge to fight
the monster underneath the bed.
The boogeyman disguised as
tropes, stereotypes, and
microaggressions are the real threat.

What if

Your thirst for knowledge
would be quenched.
Your inquisitiveness wouldn't
be met with an inquisition.

What if

Equipping yourself with more
[information] than you were given
becomes the priority.
Bettering yourself would
be the way you viewed
walking into manhood.

What if

Instead of being dropped off
on its doorstep without knowing
if your knocks would be answered.
Or if your senses
would be ready for
what's on the other side,
when you turn the knob.

What if
    Any conversation with
    opposing views would
    be considered discourse.
    Your emotions behind
    any topic would be seen
    as a passion for
    what you believe in,
      not anger toward the world.

What if
A world that allows you to
introduce yourself after
you've been able to decide
who you are.

What if
    A decision you were only
    able to make because you
    were allowed to become a man,
    not forced to be one.

Emancipation

Emancipation from what should never have been.

Celebration for the past and present
shaping things as they are and as they will be.

Honoring those who came before us
as we create legacies for those to come.

Embracing each other in uplifting love.

Liberation from if you know you know to
if you do know share with each other
    so we can learn and grow together.

Possible Thoughts

It's possible to
walk on a crowded sidewalk

and be alone in your thoughts.

  Each passerby craving for
your attention.
  Each conversation begging for
your input.
  Each step drifting you further
into seclusion.

It's possible to
walk on an empty sidewalk

*and be crowded
with your thoughts.*

Each mistake craving for
your attention.
Each argument begging for
a reply.
Each step drifting you further
away from happiness.

It's possible to

*walk in peace
with the comfort
of your thoughts.*

I Wonder

I wonder if tomorrow
will bring the start of
everything I couldn't
accomplish today

or yesterday.

I know it isn't promised
but I can't fight this feeling
that tomorrow
will be **THE** day.

*I even wonder if when
tomorrow gets here,
I will look at the new
yesterday with the
same thoughts
I had today.*

Or will I keep
looking forward to
the next day
and the next day?

Expecting an
experience
better than
the day before.

I wonder if I made
a promise to myself,
would I keep it?

> *I wonder if I promised*
> *myself tomorrow would*
> I appreciate it

even more?

A Poem for Tomorrow,
Today

Take this with you,
just in case.
Joy is an endless journey
that you've decided to take.

Gratitude is a promise
you've decided to make.

Take this with you, just in case.

Life is full of lessons,
so we learn to take the
bad with the good.

You've made it this far.
You were never a failure,
just sometimes misunderstood.

*Take this with you,
just in case.*

Embrace all of life's changes.
They're beautiful as a collective,
like a beautiful bouquet.

This is a poem for tomorrow,
but take it with you today.

*Take this with you,
just in case.*

Black Love

Black Love isn't just an ebony adjective.
It's **deeper** than the melanin in our skin.

Black love is a representation of **the strength that exists** when Black men and women come together.

Strength that **breaks** the strongholds of discrimination and **lifts** the heaviness of oppositions.

It's the model of resilience and
influential progress in our communities.
Black Love is about excellence and legacy.

Black Love is iconic like Ruby Dee and Ossie Davis.
Standing the **test of time**, inequality, and injustices.
Showing the world **that love exists** inside of being Black.

Showing the world that **love exists** even if it doesn't love us back.

Black Love is **presidential** like Barack and Michele Obama.
The royal family for the culture.
A world example of what it looks like when we love our families.
Daughters having the example of what it's like to be treated like a lady.

Shown that respect is a crown fit for a queen.

Black Love is nostalgic like grandfathers and grandmothers.

The leaders of the family. The pillars of the community.
A time when the community was family,
and it was love that held it together.
Fifty-eight years until death did my grandparents part,
but their love is a legacy that lives on.

It's a love that exemplifies family
as the cornerstone of Black Love.

It's not a movement to be anti-everyone else,
but a lifestyle that unapologetically
celebrates who we are.

The most important component to
anything with substance is the foundation.
So, when it comes to Black Love or any love,
self-love is that **foundation**.

Not just a love for your skin tone,
facial features, or the texture of your hair.
It's **loving the person you are**
in the inside as well as the outside.

It's truly knowing your value
without anyone else's validation.
Self-love is influential when it comes to the
type of people we're attracted to and
the types of relationship we get into.

We can't pour from an empty cup.
We can't truly love someone else
unless we love ourselves.

We can't fully receive love
without knowing first-hand
what love feels like.
We must trust ourselves
enough to love and to be loved.

Having examples of love allows us to love optimistically.
Being a part of love allows us to love intentionally.
Black Love is knowing and being comfortable with
who we are so that we can love without limits or restraints.

Black Love is a phenomenon
that's the fabric of our past, present,

and future.

Resilient

Sometimes I remind myself of how far
I've come and what I overcame.
Not for vanity or pride,
but to realize how much further
I can go.

Challenges are hurdles
intended for me to jump higher,
not roadblocks set up to imprison me
with the convictions of my faults.

Though the path may have changed,
as long as I'm stepping in the right direction,
the journey remains the same.

With my heart as the map
and God as my guide,
I keep pushing forward
with a passion that's

resilient and true.

Our Excellence Is Everywhere

There are hidden treasures
waiting for the chance
at discovery.

The rose that grows
from the rich unseen soil
underneath the concrete.
Against the odds.
Fighting upwards through broken paths.
Embracing its beauty.
Claiming its place in the sunlight.

The diamond that
shines brilliantly
beneath the rough.

Waiting for a grand
acknowledgment of
its brilliance.

Pure and unaltered by
the conditions of
its environment.

A splendor unrecognizable
through cloudy tainted lenses.
Where you least expect it.
In unlikely places.
Our excellence is everywhere.

Touch the Stars

Hold tight to the
things worth saving.
Let go of the
things without substance.
Grab all of the
things worth collecting.

Pay attention to how
they feel and the
feelings that they bring.
Sense the beginning
when it feels like the end.

Touch the stars
on your way to
the moon.

Discovery

Barely scratching
        the surface we still
                illuminate any room.

Peeling back our layers,
      we discover who
           we thought we were
                was only an introduction
                      to someone else.

                      Discovery never ends
              when we stop trying
        to be who everyone else
      expects us to be and
start turning the pages
            to find our own answers.

Echoes of the Past

Sometimes I can
hear the echoes of
my past mistakes.

Each time the sound
fades further and further
into the distance.

Drowned out
by the laughter
of my present
and future.

Distant memories
don't always equal
a forgotten past.

What doesn't kill us
makes us stronger,
but what we give power
controls us.

What has our ear
controls our destiny.

What has our heart
controls our soul.

And
whatever has our
attention steers us
in its direction.

Walk it Off (Keep Going)

We've been stumbling since
the day we began walking.

Learning how to get up
and keep going after each stumble.
After every near fall.

Egos more bruised than bodies.

> **Keep getting up.**
> **Keep going.**

When we learned how to run
the stumbles became falls.
A few scrapes and cuts here.
A sprain or two there.

> **Keep getting up.**
> **Walk it off.**

When we get knocked down
we get up and walk it off.
But after enough times we
become numb to the feeling.

Hiding our emotional limps
as we walk through life.
Ignoring the scars and bruises.
Never examining the pain,
just getting up and walking with it.

Limping unnoticed we
believe everything is okay.
Until we're unable to hide the limp
and it becomes an undeniable
stagger through life.

If we don't learn how to
pause and process our pain.
If we never assess the damage,
we will never be able to heal.

Keep getting up.
Keep healing

Black Owned

See me for who I am.
    I am not your assumptions. See beyond your prejudice.

See beyond your hate.

SEE BEYOND YOUR FEAR.

See beyond the negative media narratives.

See me as I am.

See me as a Black man.
                      See that I am not a threat.

Terrance P. Elmore

See a Son.
See a Brother.

See a Husband.
See a Father.

See a Grandfather.
See an Uncle.

See a Friend.

See a Neighbor.

See a Coworker.

See an Educator.

See a Veteran.

See a Human Being.

See skin that is
Black Owned

Plentiful Fruit

Forgotten trees bear a plentiful fruit
Ambitious on the leaves and ambitious at the root
Black excellence thrivin' in the hidden feeds
Plentiful fruit growing from the mahogany trees

Picturesque scene of Black girl magic and Black boy joy
Euphoria that ignorance and hate cannot destroy
Scent of resilience sweet and fresh
Gadsdens Wharf now a symbol of progress

Here is a fruit for a rewritten anthology
For the timelines to trend
For the world to see
For the twisted plot
For the stereotypes to stop
Here is a plentiful and ambitious crop

Uncompromised by those strange and familiar fruits
Encourgaged by growth and structure through the
Intersection of trauma and triumph

About the Author

Terrance P. Elmore is a South Carolina native and Benedict College graduate who's doing his part to spread love in a world that seems to be full of hate; one poem, one podcast, and one message at a time. He's the author of "Love Letters: A Collection of Poems" and "The Essence of Love." Both poetry collections are centered around love because he recognized a need to distinguish the difference between real love and misrepresented love. The main focus of his poetry is love, hope, and inspiration because that's something the world could use more of.

His love for writing began at an early age, but outside of the classroom, it wasn't something that many people knew. He always loved writing assignments and looked forward to county writing tests. His love for poetry started shaping when he learned about Langston Hughes and The Harlem Renaissance. As an adult, he continued to write poems, but it still wasn't something that many people knew until he decided to create a poetry blog and publish his first book.

The Brown Sugar Cafe Podcast is his latest contribution to this mission. The Brown Sugar Café blog is a place where poetry meets the heart and The Brown Sugar Café podcast is the place where poetry meets conversation.

To see what's next make sure to subscribe to TheBrownSugarCafe.blog and The Brown Sugar Café Podcast. Join him on his journey to spread love in a world that seems to be full of hate.

www.TheBrownSugarCafe.Blog/links

@TheBrownSugarCafe